SPECTRUM WRITING
by Iris Schwartz

P9-BJJ-392

CONTENTS

1997 © McGraw-Hill Learning Materials

Project Editor: Sandra Kelley
Text: Design and Production by Harry Chester Associates
        Illustrated by Connie Maltese

Things To Remember About Writing

WRITING

- Be sure that every story you write has a main idea.
- Write directions and story parts in order.
- Use order words like <u>first</u> and <u>next</u>.
- Use <u>er</u> and <u>est</u> to compare things.
- Use your senses to describe something.
- If you write a story problem, then tell how the problem was solved.
- Choose clear nouns and describing words.
- Write the first word of a sentence with a capital letter.
- Write names, days of the week, and the word <u>I</u> with capital letters.
- Proofread your work to make it better.

unit 1
Writing Main Ideas

The **main idea** tells what the whole thing is about.

 Be sure that every story you write has a main idea.

Choose a title that tells the main idea of a picture or story.

Choose clear nouns when you write.

Finding the right group

A. Bob has three jobs. He cleans. He cooks. He fixes things. Help Bob group what he needs for each job. Use the picture. Write the name of each tool under the right group.

Tools for Cleaning	Tools for Cooking	Tools for Fixing

B. Look at the groups in each picture. Find the name of each group. Then write the name in a sentence under the picture. One is done for you.

| animals | shapes | games | plants |

This is a group of animals.

_____

_____

_____

C. Look at the groups below. Cross out what does not belong. Then write the name of the group under each picture.

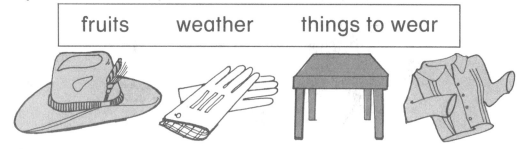

fruits	weather	things to wear

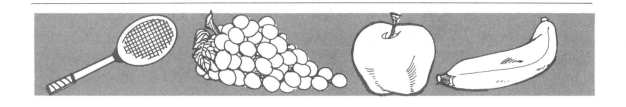

D. Read each list of words. Then write the group name on the line above the list.

Meals	Money	Colors

_____	_____	_____
pink	penny	breakfast
brown	dime	lunch
gold	dollar	supper

Write these groups on a piece of paper. Draw three pictures that belong to each group.

Jobs	Things with Wheels	Food

Writing the main idea of a picture

The **main idea** tells what the whole picture is about.

A. Look at each picture below. Underline the sentence that tells the main idea.

Cities have buildings.

Maps are useful.

A moon person visits Earth.

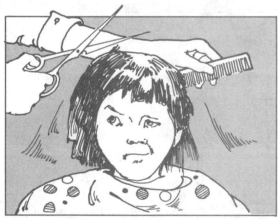

Jean has brown hair.

Jean gets a bad haircut.

Jean sits in a chair.

Corn is on the table.

Winning can make you sick.

A sign is on the wall.

B. Look at each picture. Write the main idea under the picture. Tell what the whole picture is about.

_____

_____

_____

_____

_____

_____

_____

_____

C. Draw a picture below. Then write the main idea on the line.

[Empty box for drawing]

_____

_____

 Take two pieces of paper. Draw a picture on each paper. Then write the main idea under each picture.

Writing the main idea of a story

The main idea of a story tells what the whole story is about.

A. Read each story. Then underline the sentence that tells the main idea.

Carlos is talking into the banana. He says he is doing well. He says he is feeling fine. He says he will call back tomorrow. Why does Carlos talk into a banana? A real call costs too much money.

The main idea of this story is
    Carlos feels fine.
    Bananas are good.
    Carlos makes a free call.

I love my brown shoes. I can tap dance in them. I can kick a can with them. But mostly, I can stamp in mud with them. And Dad can never guess.

The main idea of this story is
    Here is how to buy shoes.
    Brown shoes are fun.
    Let's play kick the can.

I got my raincoat. Mom found a rain hat. Brother pulled on boots. Finally, Grandpa put Frisky in the tub. Our dog sure hates a bath.

The main idea of this story is
    We walk in the rain.
    Frisky is helpful.
    The family gives Frisky a bath.

B. Read the story. Then write the main idea.

Dotty went to a park with her friends. There were rides that went up and down. There were rides that went around and around. There were even rides that went over and under. Dotty loved all these rides. But now she cannot stand up straight.

_____

_____

B. Read the story. Then write the main idea.

Uncle Emilio gave Anna a lucky penny. He wanted her to have a lucky day. But that night Anna said that nothing lucky happened.

"Did an elephant eat your lunch?" asked Uncle Emilio.

"No," said Anna.

"Did a tiger take your hat?" asked Uncle Emilio.

"No," said Anna.

"Well then," laughed Uncle Emilio. "It was a lucky day for you after all."

_____

_____

C. Choose one of the main ideas below. Draw a line under it. Then write a story that tells about your main idea.

Some days everything goes wrong.
There is one food I really love.
I once played a funny joke.

_____

_____

_____

_____

 Choose a different main idea from **C.** Or think of your own. Then write a story that tells about your main idea. Use another piece of paper.

Writing a title

A **title** is a name for a picture or a story. It tells the main idea of the picture or story.

A. Look at the picture below. Draw a line under the best title for the picture.

A good title for this picture is

    Magic Shows Are Fun
    Skunks Make Great Pets
    Sometimes Tricks Go Wrong

A. Draw a line under the best title for the picture.

A good title for this picture is
  Donna Saves Her Snowballs
  Donna Gets Lunch
  Donna Wears Gloves

B. Read the story below. Find the best title. Then write it on the line above the story.

_____

Yesterday our class went to visit an old lady. We had to take a boat. We waited in a long line. Lots of people took her picture. She was very tall and kind of green. This is a true story. Here is my picture to prove it.

A good title for this story is
  Helping Old People
  Fun at the Zoo
  A Visit to a Lady

C. Read the story below. Think of a good title. Write it above the story.

_____

    Tom saved whatever he got. He saved string if he got some. He saved bottle caps when he got them. Then Tom thought of something new to save. He ran upstairs and downstairs. He ran all over the place. What was Tom saving now? He was saving time!

D. Choose one of the titles below. Or think of your own. Write the title on the top line. Then write a story that fits the title.

> A Man Makes a Six-Foot Sandwich
> A Strange Animal Is Found
> A Family Takes a Trip

_____

_____

_____

_____

_____

_____

Choose a different title from **D.** Or think of your own. Then write a story that fits your title.

Choosing clear nouns

The <u>thing</u> sees the <u>person</u>.   The <u>glob</u> sees the <u>teacher</u>.

The nouns in the second sentence are clear. They give a better picture of what is happening.

A. Read each sentence. Look at the underlined nouns. Think of clearer nouns. Write them on the lines. Then draw a clear picture about the sentence.

1. The <u>person</u> feeds the <u>thing</u>.

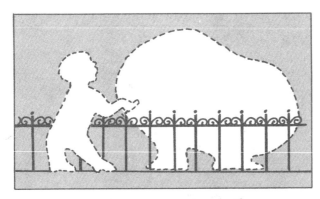

The _____ feeds the _____.

2. The <u>person</u> paints a <u>thing</u>.

 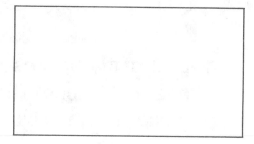

The _____ paints a _____.

3. The <u>person</u> builds a <u>thing</u>.

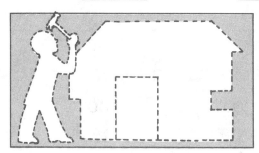 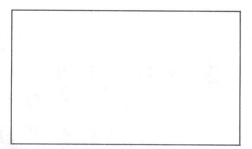

The _____ builds a _____.

B. Look at the underlined nouns. Fill in the sentences with clearer nouns. Your sentences can be funny.

1. The <u>animal</u> eats its <u>thing</u>.

The _____ eats its _____.

2. The <u>person</u> likes the <u>place</u>.

The _____ likes the _____.

3. The <u>animal</u> plays the <u>thing</u>.

The _____ plays the _____.

 Write <u>person</u>, <u>place</u>, and <u>thing</u> on three pieces of paper. Try to write four clear nouns for each word. Then write sentences using your nouns.

1. Look at the pictures in this group. Cross out what does not belong. Then write the name of the group under the pictures.

_____

2. Read the story. Then write the main idea.

    Jenny and I watched a scary TV show. I laughed at it. I wasn't scared at all. Then Jenny said, "Look! The TV isn't plugged in!"

_____

3. Look at the picture below. Write a title for it.

_____

4. Look at the underlined nouns. Fill in the sentence with clearer nouns.

    The <u>person</u> sat on the <u>thing</u>.

The _____ sat on the _____

unit 2
Writing in Sequence

Sequence means order.

 Use order words like <u>first</u> and <u>next</u> in sentences.

Write "how to" directions in order.

Write story parts in order.

Write the first word of a sentence with a capital letter.

Write names, days of the week, and the word <u>I</u> with capital letters.

Writing picture stories

A. Look at the groups of pictures. They can tell a story. But they are not in order. Write <u>first</u>, <u>next</u>, and <u>last</u> under each picture to show the right order. The first one is done for you.

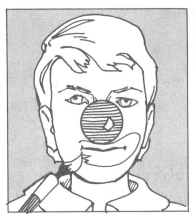  

   next   first   last

_____ _____ _____

Pictures that are in order tell a story.

B. Look at the pictures below. They tell part of a story. Finish the story by drawing the last picture.

First   Next   Last

First   Next   Last

C. The pictures below tell part of a story. Finish the story by drawing the last picture. Then write a sentence that tells about each picture.

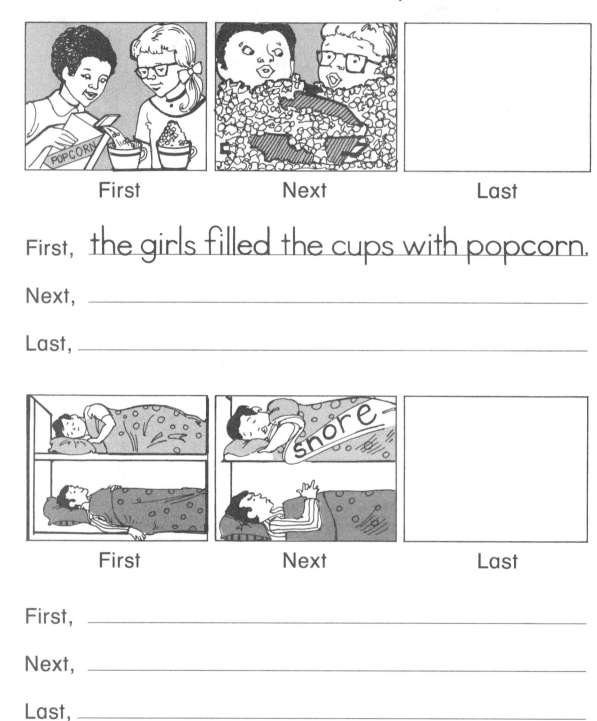

First   Next   Last

First, the girls filled the cups with popcorn.

Next, _____

Last, _____

First   Next   Last

First, _____

Next, _____

Last, _____

 Draw your own picture story on a piece of paper. Draw three pictures in order. Write a sentence that tells about each picture.

Using order words

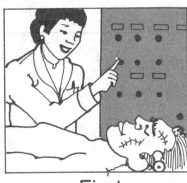

First   Next   Finally

<u>First</u>, I press a button.
<u>Next</u>, I see him move.
<u>Finally</u>, my monster and I play basketball.

The underlined words are **order words**. They tell the order in which things happen.

A. Put the sentences in order. Write the order words that are under the pictures in front of the right sentences.

First   Next   Last

_____, something pulled on his line.

_____, Andy fell into the water.

_____, Andy was fishing.

A. Make the sentences match the pictures. Put the order words that are under the pictures in front of the right sentence.

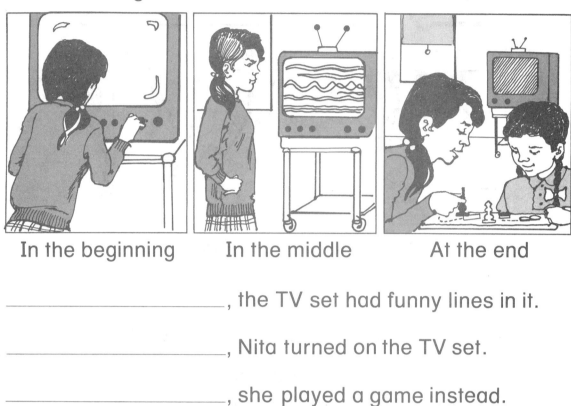

In the beginning   In the middle   At the end

_____, the TV set had funny lines in it.

_____, Nita turned on the TV set.

_____, she played a game instead.

In the morning   In the afternoon   In the evening

_____, Mr. Jones went home.

_____, Mr. Jones was reading the news.

_____, he did not see the spaceship come.

You can use order words to help tell a story.

B. Write three sentences to tell a story about each picture. Use the order words to tell the order in which things happen.

First   Second   Third

First, the donuts have no holes.

_____

_____

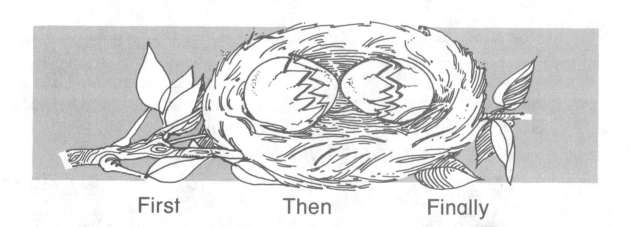

First   Then   Finally

_____

_____

_____

Choose one set of three order words from **A** or **B**. Write your own story. Use the order words to tell the order in which things happen.

Writing "how to" directions

Directions can tell how to make or do something.

A. Write directions for making a jack-o'-lantern. Use order words to start your sentences.

First

Next

Finally

First, get a pumpkin.

_____

_____

B. Write directions for joining the library. Use order words to start your sentences.

First

Second

Third

_____

_____

_____

Directions can tell how to go somewhere.

C. Help Long John find the treasure. Write directions for him. Use order words.

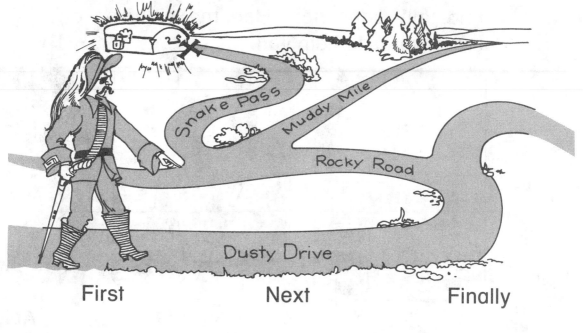

First   Next   Finally

_____

_____

_____

Directions can tell how to use something.

D. Write the directions for brushing your teeth. Use order words in your sentences.

First   Then   Last

_____

_____

_____

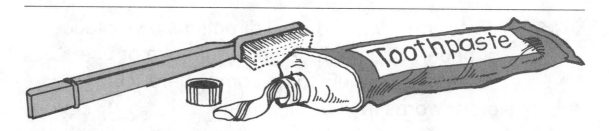

Directions can tell how to make food. These directions are called a **recipe.**

E. Write directions for making a peanut butter and jelly sandwich. Use the pictures and order words to help you.

First   Next   At last

_____

_____

_____

F. Write your own directions. Tell how to make a telephone call. Use order words to write your directions.

_____

_____

_____

Write your own "how to" directions on a piece of paper. You might tell how to make or use something or how to go somewhere. Use order words in your directions.

Writing story parts in order

All stories have a **beginning**, a **middle**, and an **end**.

A. Read each story below. Then write <u>beginning</u>, <u>middle</u>, or <u>end</u> in front of each sentence. The first one is done for you.

middle   But we laughed because the sun was out.

end   Later our picnic lunch got wet.

beginning   Ms. Weather said it would rain.

_____ Then he thought of how he could help.

_____ A whale wanted to help people.

_____ Finally, he opened up a swim school.

_____ At last, she put the carrot top in her hat.

_____ Next she put the carrot in her mouth.

_____ First, Jenny pulled a carrot from the ground.

B. Each story below has a beginning and a middle. Write your own end for each story.

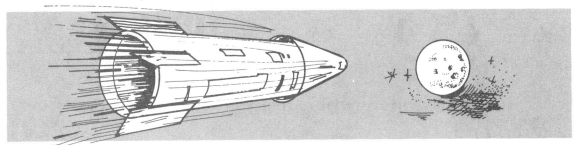

1. Mandy took a spaceship to the moon.
   But she could not find a place to land.

   So she _____

   _____

2. Henry saw a monster movie on TV.
   He said he was not scared.

   But that night _____

   _____

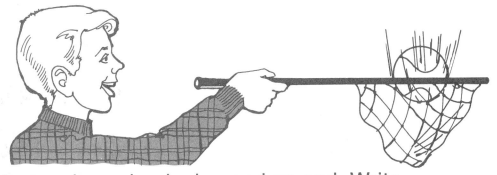

C. Each story has a beginning and an end. Write your own middle for each story.

It was Benny's turn to catch.

But Benny _____

_____

So now he uses a butterfly net.

Poor Gus was lost on an island.

So he _____

_____

Finally, he got home.

D. The story below has a middle and an end.
Write your own beginning for the story.

Olga _____

_____

Her balloon got bigger and bigger.
Pop! Olga's balloon was gone.

Write a story with three sentences on a piece
of paper. Your three sentences should tell the
beginning, middle, and end of your story.

lesson

Using capital letters

The first word of a sentence begins with a capital letter.

A. Write three sentences about the picture below. Begin each sentence with a capital letter. One sentence has been written for you.

The boy puts on a funny nose.

Names of persons and pets begin with capital letters.

B. Give everyone in this picture a name. Then write a sentence about what each one is doing. Begin each name with a capital letter.

David _____ _____

David is eating some watermelon.

_____

_____

_____

The names of the days of the week begin with capital letters. The word <u>I</u> begins with a capital letter.

C. Read each sentence. Then draw a circle around each word that should begin with a capital letter.

1. On tuesday, i played baseball.

2. On wednesday, i went swimming.

3. On thursday, i did the shopping.

4. On friday, i did my homework.

5. On saturday, i slept late.

Write On Write a sentence for each day of the week. Tell what you like to do each day. Or tell what you did each day last week.

1. Look at the pictures. Write <u>first</u>, <u>next</u>, and <u>last</u> under each picture to tell the right order.

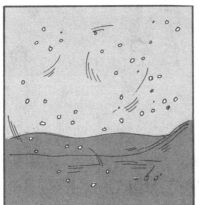  

a._____ b._____ c._____

2. Read this story. Write your own middle.

    a.   Nina's cat was lost.

    b. _____

    c.   Nina's cat is home again.

3. Write directions telling how to mail a postcard.
Use order words to begin your directions.

_____

_____

_____

4. Read the sentences below. Then draw a circle around each word that should begin with a capital letter.

    a.   my sister and i like to play catch.

    b.   ron gave jamie a birthday present.

unit 3
Writing Comparisons

When you **compare** things, you tell how they are the same or different.

 Use <u>er</u> and <u>than</u> to compare two things.

Add <u>er</u> or <u>est</u> to a word to compare three things.

Use <u>like</u> or <u>as</u> to compare different things.

Use describing words to tell exactly what you mean.

Comparing two pictures

When you **compare** things, you tell how they are the same or different.

A. Look at each picture. Then fill in the sentences. Use the words in the box to compare the two things. One has been done for you.

taller than
shorter than

Loony is ___taller than___ Moony.

Moony is ___shorter than___ Loony.

faster than
slower than

A bike is _____ a car.

A car is _____ a bike.

younger than
older than

Van is _____ Dan.

Dan is _____ Van.

softer than
harder than

Books are _____ a pillow.

A pillow is _____ books.

B. Write sentences to compare the things in each picture. Use the words in the box.

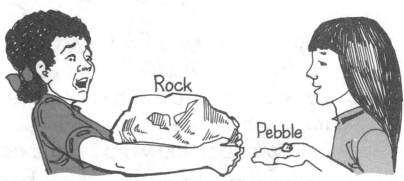

lighter than
heavier than

A pebble is lighter than a rock.

A rock is heavier than a pebble.

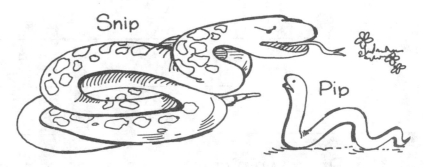

longer than
shorter than

_____

_____

B. Write sentences that compare.

bigger than
smaller than

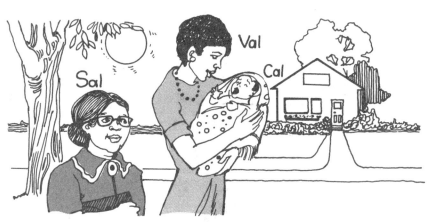

_____

_____

C. Look at the picture. Think of ways to compare the people. Then write four sentences that compare. Use the words in the boxes.

| taller than | younger than | louder than | lighter than |
| shorter than | older than | softer than | heavier than |

_____

_____

_____

_____

 Draw two pictures on a piece of paper. Think of ways to compare your pictures. You may use the words in the boxes in **A** or **B**. Write three sentences that compare the pictures.

2 Comparing three pictures

You can use one word to compare three things. You add **er** or **est** to the word.

A. Compare the animals below. Use the words in each box. Finish each sentence. The first one has been done for you.

long	longer	longest

Ty is _long_.

Hy is _longer_.

Sly is _longest_.

large	larger	largest

Tess is _____.

Bess is _____.

Fess is _____.

small	smaller	smallest

Mack is _____.

Zack is _____.

Jack is _____.

B. Write three sentences about each picture. Use the words in the box to compare the three people. One is started for you.

strong
stronger
strongest

Ed is strong.

_____

_____

tall
taller
tallest

_____

_____

Some words end in <u>y</u>. Change <u>y</u> to <u>i</u> before
you add <u>er</u> or <u>est</u>.

C. Write three sentences. Use the words in the
box to compare the three people or animals.

silly
sillier
silliest

_____

_____

_____

tiny
tinier
tiniest

_____

_____

_____

 Draw three things on a piece of paper.
Choose a word to describe these things. Add
<u>er</u> and <u>est</u> to your word. Then write three
sentences that compare the three things.

Comparing with like and as

Betty turns <u>as</u> white <u>as</u> a sheet.
Betty looks <u>like</u> a white sheet.

Another way to compare things is to use <u>like</u> or <u>as</u>. These words tell about one thing by comparing it to another. The sentences above compare Betty to a white sheet.

A. Look at each picture. Read each sentence beginning. Then circle the best word to finish the sentence. Write the word on both lines.

glass
wood

The water is as clear as _____.

The water is like _____.

water
mud

The breakfast food is as thick as _____.

The breakfast food is like _____.

B. Look at the pictures below. Finish each sentence. Use the words from the boxes.

a cook at lunchtime
an apartment house

The man's foot is as big as _____.

Joe is working like _____.

an ant hill
a silver bird

The town looks as tiny as _____.

A plane is like _____.

C. Look at the picture. Then finish the sentences. Write your own comparing words.

The sun is like _____.

The sky is as blue as _____.

The water is like _____.

I swim just like a _____.

Oh, no! My skin is as red as _____.

 Draw a place you would like to be at. Think of things to compare your place to. Then write two sentences below your picture. Use <u>like</u> or <u>as</u> in each sentence.

lesson 4

Comparing people

When you compare people, you show how they are the same or different. You can compare how people look.

A. Look at the pictures below. Use the words in the boxes to compare the sizes of the people. Write a sentence about each person.

tall
short

Rex   Tex

heavy
thin

Rex is short and heavy.

Tex is tall and thin.

Minnie   Winnie

B. Look at the pictures below. Use the words in the boxes to compare what the people are wearing. Write a sentence about each person.

| jacket |
| shorts |

| cap |
| tie |

_____

_____

| dress |
| pants |

| cap |
| gloves |

_____

_____

You can also compare what people say or do.

C. Look at the pictures. Read the sentences. Then tell which person is speaking.

Art_____ : What beautiful, perfect fruit.

Bart_____ : I want to eat this fruit.

_____: Fishing is fun.

_____: I do not know why anyone likes to fish.

_____: I love snow.

_____: I wish it were spring.

Think of two people. They can be people you know or made-up people. Write two or three sentences about each person. Are they the same or different? Compare how they look. Tell what they wear. Then write a sentence for each one to say to the other.

Using describing words

Which dog does Gina want? She should use describing words to tell which dog she wants. She could say: "I want to buy that tiny, spotted dog." <u>Tiny</u> and <u>spotted</u> are describing words. They tell which dog she wants.

A. Use the describing words in the boxes to tell exactly what you want.

| long striped |  | short spotted |

I want to buy the _____, _____ snake.

| big floppy |   | small feathered |

I want to buy the _____, _____ hat.

B. Use the describing words in the boxes to tell what you want. Write a sentence for each.

| clean neat | | dirty torn |

| new shiny | | old dented |

 **C.** Pretend that you are a salesperson in a store. How would you get the man in the picture to buy the cap? Use the describing words in the box. Write three sentences to sell the cap.

| good-looking | comfortable | warm |
| striped | different | |

This cap is surely different.

_____

_____

_____

 Draw something on a piece of paper. List describing words under your picture. Then write three sentences about the picture. Use your describing words in your sentences.

Post-Test

1. Look at the picture below. Finish each comparing sentence.

| bright |
| brighter |
| brightest |

The candle is _____.

The lamp is _____.

The sun is _____.

2. Look at the picture below. Compare the two people.

| busy |
| lazy |

BETH   SETH

_____

_____

3. Finish these sentences.

   a. My nose is as red as a _____

   b. Max is as strong as a _____.

4. Write two describing words for this dog.

_____ , _____

48

unit 4
Writing Details

Details are small parts that make a whole.

 Use your senses to describe something.

Use describing words to tell how a person looks.

When you write an ad, use exciting words to get people interested.

Use words that tell <u>how</u>, <u>when</u>, and <u>where</u> in your writing.

1

Writing with your senses

You learn about things by <u>seeing</u>, <u>hearing</u>, <u>smelling</u>, <u>tasting</u>, and <u>touching</u>. These are called the **five senses.**

A. Write answers to these questions about the picture above.

1. What sense is Molly using? _____

2. What are the senses poor Polly is using?

_____

B. Look at the pictures below. Write the senses you could use to learn about each thing.

_____

_____

_____

_____

C. Look at the pictures below. Circle the senses you could use to learn about each thing. Then write two sentences to describe the thing. Use the describing words in the box. Or think of your own. One has been done for you.

red	sweet	crunching	dry
cold	delicious	thundering	colored
noisy	rushing	scattered	drifting

 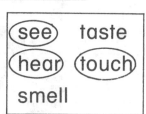

see   taste
hear touch
smell

(circled: see, hear, touch)

I see a rushing train.

I hear

see   taste
hear touch
smell

see   taste
hear touch
smell

D. Look at the picture below. The people in this movie house are using many senses. Write four sentences to describe what is happening. Use a sense word in each sentence.

see	hear	smell	taste	touch

_____

_____

_____

_____

 Choose a place you like to be. Draw a picture of this place on a piece of paper. List the senses you can use in your place. Then write at least three sentences about your picture. Use a sense word in each sentence.

Writing about a person

When you describe a person, you can tell how the person looks.

A. You can use many words to tell about a person. Words can tell about size, hair, and what a person is wearing. Look at the words in the box. Write each word under what it describes. Some words may fit in two places.

tall	short	hat	dark
curly	pants	fat	gloves
thin	long	straight	tie
dress	shirt	light	shorts

Size	Hair	Wearing
_____	_____	_____
_____	_____	_____
_____	_____	_____
_____	_____	_____
	_____	_____
	_____	_____

B. Describe the hair of the people below. Write a sentence about each person. Use at least two describing words from **A** in each sentence.

The King _____

The Queen _____

The Prince _____

C. Look at the picture. Use the words under the boxes to describe what the people are wearing. Write three sentences.

striped   plaid   checked   flowered   polka dot

_____

_____

_____

D. Mr. Lobo and his class are on a trip. Choose three people to describe. You may use the words in **A** and **C**. Or think of your own words.

_____

_____

_____

_____

_____

Think about someone you know well.
Describe the person on a piece of paper.
Write at least three sentences. Use the words
in this lesson. Or think of your own words.

Writing riddles

The story above is a **riddle.** It has sentences that describe something. It asks you to guess what is being described.

A. Read the riddle below. Choose the best answer in the box. Then write it on the line.

I can make people laugh.
Chickens grow me all over.
People put me in their hats.

| an egg |
| a feather |
| a joke |

I am ⎯⎯⎯⎯⎯⎯⎯⎯⎯.

B. Read the riddle below. Then write the answer to the riddle.

I look like a little dot of light.
You can see me when the sky is dark.
Children often make a wish on me.

I am ⎯⎯⎯⎯⎯⎯⎯⎯⎯.

C. Look at the pictures below. Write a riddle for each one. Use the words in the box to describe it. Or think of your own words.

a rabbit

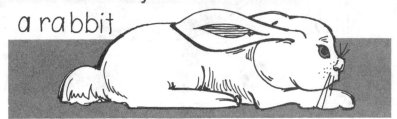

ears
tail
hop
pet

I have long ears but a short tail.

When I move, I hop.

I might be someone's pet.

I am a rabbit.

an egg

white
yellow
shell
crack

_____

_____

_____

I am an egg.

a rainbow

colors
beautiful
rain
across

_____

_____

_____

I am a rainbow.

C. Write a riddle for the picture.

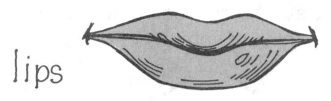

lips

red
smile
kiss
whistle

_____

_____

_____

I am your lips.

D. Choose one of the things below. Write a riddle
about it. First describe your thing. Then tell
what it is.

bank

needle

fire

skateboard

_____

_____

_____

I am _____ .

Draw something on a piece of paper. Then
write sentences describing your picture. Read
your riddle to the class. See if anyone can
guess what you drew.

Writing an ad

An **ad** gets people to buy something or do something. Ads use exciting words to get people interested.

Read the ad below. The underlined words are exciting words. They get you interested.

Got those Sunday blues?

Come to <u>Wonder</u> Village!
A <u>fun-packed</u> park for kids
With <u>daring rides</u> and <u>great games</u>
A park of <u>prizes</u> — and <u>surprises</u>

Wonder Village —
You'll <u>wish Sundays
never ended.</u>

A. Read the following ad. Underline the exciting words that get you interested.

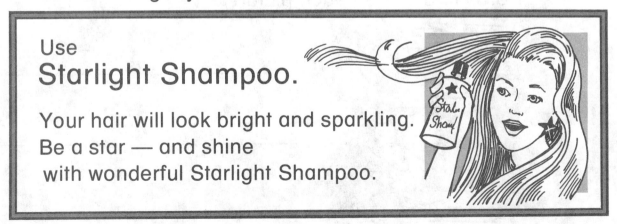

Use
Starlight Shampoo.

Your hair will look bright and sparkling.
Be a star — and shine
with wonderful Starlight Shampoo.

B. Look at the ad below. Write an exciting word on each line. Use the words in the box. Or think of your own.

delicious	fruity	sweet	mouth-watering
yummy	crunchy	tasty	good for you

Tired of Sticky Candy?

Change to Fruit on a Stick!

Fruit Sticks are _____ and _____.

They are _____ and _____ too.

Friends will say, " _____!"

C. Look at the pictures below. Write two exciting words to describe each picture.

_____ _____

_____ _____

_____ _____

D. A great new breakfast food is shown below. Write an ad for it. Use some of the exciting words in the box. Or think of your own. Try to get people to buy this food.

crispy	tasty	fresh
lively	snappy	good for you

_____

_____

_____

_____

_____

Write On Choose something you would like to buy. List exciting words to describe it. Use these words to write an ad. Draw a picture for your ad.

Telling how, when, and where

Some words tell <u>how</u>, <u>when</u>, and <u>where</u>.

Max skates <u>carelessly</u> <u>indoors</u> <u>today</u>.

A. Use the sentence above to answer these questions.

1. Which word tells <u>how</u> Max skates? _____

2. Which word tells <u>when</u> Max skates? _____

3. Which word tells <u>where</u> Max skates? _____

B. Read the sentences below. Underline the words that tell how, when, and where.

1. Yesterday, Mike had a picnic outdoors.

2. He carefully spread a blanket.

3. Soon he was happily eating his sandwich.

4. Suddenly he heard a loud buzzing overhead.

5. Today Mike is calmly eating his sandwich indoors.

C. Write words to finish each sentence below. The words under the line tell you which kind of word to write. Use some of the words in the box. Or think of your own.

how	when	where
quickly	later	inside
slowly	tomorrow	outside
loudly	next	there

1. My ball tells what will happen _____.
   <u>when</u>

2. You will hear someone knock _____
   at your door.
                                               <u>how</u>

3. You will walk _____ to the door.
                       <u>how</u>

4. A tall person will be _____ with a letter.
                              <u>where</u>

5. You will take the letter _____.
                              <u>where</u>

6. Then you will _____ read, "Happy Birthday."
                     <u>how</u>

Write a story about something funny that happened to you. Use words in your sentences to tell how, when, and where.

Post-Test

1. Write the senses you can use to describe the things below.

a. flower_____

b. star_____

see taste
hear touch
smell

2. Look at the picture. Write a sentence about each pair of boots. You may use the words in the box.

PAM   SAM

a. Pam_____

b. Sam_____

muddy old
shiny new

3. Write a riddle to describe the picture.

_____

_____

_____

I am a telephone.

4. Finish the following sentence. Tell when.

Brett will visit Ted_____.

64

unit 5
Writing About Cause and Effect

A **cause** is what makes something happen. An **effect** is what happens.

 One way to write a story is to think of a problem. Then tell how the problem was solved.

When you write a thank-you note, tell why you liked what was done for you.

Proofread your work to make it better.

Writing about cause and effect pictures

Cause

Effect

A **cause** is what makes something happen. An **effect** is what happens. Look at the picture above. What is the cause? What is the effect?

Cause: Toby put too much glue on the paper.
Effect: Toby and his cat stick to the paper.

A. Look at the pictures. Draw a line to match the cause with the effect.

Cause Effect

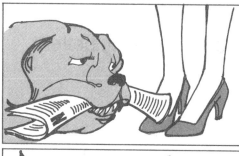

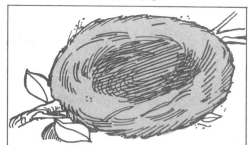

Cause	Effect

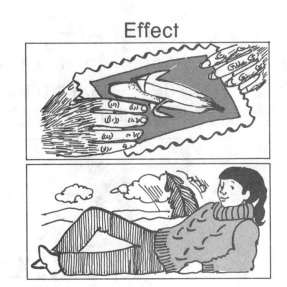

B. Look at the pictures below. Then write the cause and effect on the lines.

Cause

Effect

Cause: _____

Effect: _____

Cause

Effect

Cause: _____

Effect: _____

C. Look at each picture below. Think what will happen next. Draw a picture to show the effect. Then write the cause and effect under the pictures.

Cause

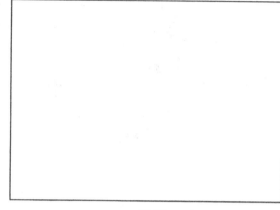

Effect

Cause: _____

Effect: _____

Cause

Effect

Cause: _____

Effect: _____

 Draw a cause picture and an effect picture. Write two sentences below your pictures. One sentence should tell the cause. The other should tell the effect.

Writing cause and effect sentences

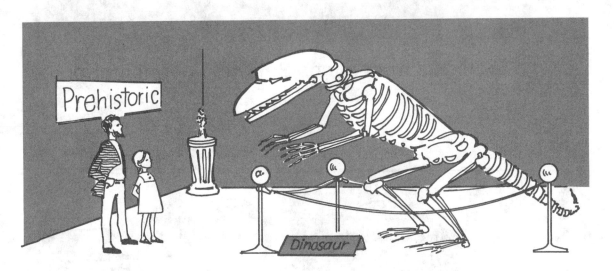

Dad took Hetty to see the dinosaur. __c__

Now Hetty says she wants one for a pet. __e__

A. Read the sentences below. Write **c** next to the sentence that tells the cause. Write **e** next to the sentence that tells the effect.

1. Manfred opened the box

   with the bow. _____
   A funny clown popped

   out. _____

2. Our sand castle was washed away. _____
   A big wave came in. _____

B. Each sentence below gives a cause. Write a sentence that tells an effect for each cause.

The lights went out as Betsy did her homework.

Effect: _____

_____

Boomer is growing bigger every day.

Effect: _____

_____

The scarecrow looks friendly.

Effect: _____

_____

C. Each sentence below gives an effect. Write a
sentence that tells a cause for each effect.

Cause: _____

_____

Effect: So we dressed up like monsters.

Cause: _____

_____

Effect: So I let it ring.

 Draw a picture on a piece of paper. Show a
cause or an effect. Then write a cause
sentence and an effect sentence.

3 Writing story problems and endings

A. Becky is going camping in a dry place. But she forgot to take water. Solve Becky's problem. Draw a line under the best answer.

Forget the water and keep walking.
Find someone who will share water.
Return to the hotel to get water.

B. Look at the pictures. Decide what the problem is in each picture. Then try to solve it. Draw a line under the best answer.

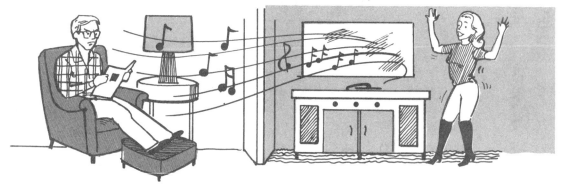

Try not to listen.
Ask her to play the music more softly.
Stop reading and start dancing.

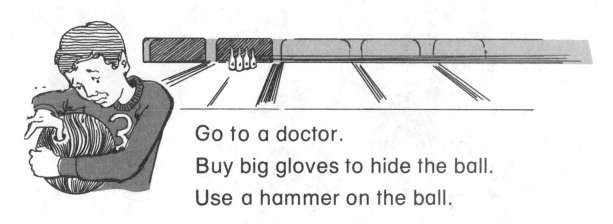

Go to a doctor.

Buy big gloves to hide the ball.

Use a hammer on the ball.

C. Look at the pictures. Write the problem you see in each picture. Then write an answer to the problem. One is started for you.

Problem: Jeff can't get on the bus.

Answer: He should

Problem: _____

Answer: _____

C. Write the problem you see. Then write an answer to the problem.

Problem: _____

Answer: _____

_____

D. Draw a picture that shows a problem. Write the problem on the line. Then write an answer to the problem.

_____

Problem: _____

Answer: _____

_____

Write a story about a problem. It can be a real or made-up problem. At the end of the story, tell how the problem was solved.

Writing a thank-you note

Say thank you when someone is nice to you.

A. Look at the pictures. Pretend you are the person in each picture. Write two sentences that say thank you. Tell why you liked what was done for you.

Thank you for this wonderful meal.
You are a great cook.

_____

_____

A. Pretend you are the woman below. Say thank you. Tell why you liked what the girl did.

_____

_____

Sometimes you may want to say thank you to someone in a note.

B. Pretend your uncle gave you this camera. Write a thank-you note to your uncle. Tell him nice things about the camera. Tell why you like it. Sign your name at the bottom.

Dear Uncle _____,

_____

_____

_____

_____

                  Love,

           _____

C. On Valentine's Day, you can write a special kind of thank-you note. Below is a Valentine's Day card. Write it to someone you care about. Thank the person for all he or she does for you. Sign your name at the bottom.

Dear _____,

_____

_____

_____

_____

_____

Love,

_____

Draw a picture of something nice someone did for you. Write a thank-you note to the person below your picture. Tell the person why you liked what was done for you. Then give that special person your thank-you note.

lesson

Proofreading

Proofreading means reading over something you have written to make it better.

A. The story below does not have capital letters. Proofread the story. Put capital letters where they belong. The first sentence shows you what to do.

    L   F   R   I

l̸ast f̸riday, r̸afael and i̸ went to the lost and

found. rafael lost his glasses on thursday.

mr. perry told us to look there. we found a

broken bike wheel. the glasses were not

there. unlucky rafael must buy new glasses.

i was luckier. i got to keep the broken wheel.

B. The story below has words that are spelled wrong. Proofread the story. Fix the words that are wrong. The first sentence shows you what to do.

      easy   make   from

It is ~~eazy~~ to ~~mak~~ a whistle ~~frum~~ a raisin box.

First, et all the raisins. Then cloz up the box.

Next, put your mouth to the box and blo hard. If

you do it rite, a loud whistle can be heard. Be

shur not to let the teacher hear this trick.

C. The story below is not very interesting. It needs exact nouns. It needs describing words. It needs words that tell how, when, and where. Write the story again. Add some interesting words. The first sentence shows you what to do.

It is fun to visit places. We went to a place. Chickens walked. A cow was there. A horse was running. A farmer gave us something. We drove around.

It is fun to visit new and exciting places.

_____

_____

_____

_____

_____

_____

_____

Write a story about a strange dream you had. Or make up a dream. Then proofread your story. Be sure you put in all the capital letters. Be sure your words are spelled right. Be sure you used interesting words.

1. Look at the pictures below. Then write the cause and effect on the line.

Cause:_____

Effect: _____

2. The sentence below gives a cause. Write a sentence that tells an effect for the cause.

Maria has a hole in her pocket.

Effect: _____

3. Look at the picture. Write the problem you see. Then write an answer to the problem.

Problem:_____

Answer:_____

4. Proofread this sentence.   chris haz a new puupi

Post-Test Answers; pg 16

1. The sun should be crossed out.
   This is a group of flowers.
2. Wording will vary. A possible answer:
   The TV was working by magic.
3. Answer will vary. A possible title: Dinner-time
4. Answers will vary. For example:
   The girl sat on the chair.

Post-Test Answers; pg 32

1. a. first   b. last   c. next
2. Answers will vary. For example:
   b. A neighbor found the cat.
3. Answers may vary slightly:
   First, write the address.
   Next, put a stamp on it.
   Last, put the card in a mail box.
4. a. *my* and *i* should be circled.
   b. *ron* and *jamie* should be circled.

Post-Test Answers; pg 48

1. The candle is <u>bright</u>.
   The lamp is <u>brighter</u>.
   The sun is <u>brightest</u>.
2. Beth is busy.
   Seth is lazy.
3. Answers will vary. Be sure that the
   children's similes compare unlike things.
4. Answers will vary. Some possibilities are
   sleepy, spotted, quiet.

Post-Test Answers; pg 64

1. a. see, smell, touch
   b. see
2. Answers will vary. Possible answers:
   a. Pam has muddy, old boots.
   b. Sam has shiny, new boots.
3. Answers will vary. One possibility:
   Sometimes I ring.
   Sometimes you talk to me.
   Sometimes you listen to me.
4. Answers will vary. At this level, accept
   one-word or phrase answers as long as
   they tell *when.*

Post-Test Answers; pg 80

1. Answers should be similar to these:
   Cause: The boy sat on wet paint.
   Effect: He has paint on his clothes.
2. Answers will vary. Maria should lose or
   drop something from her pocket.
3. Problem: The bag broke.
   Answer: Answers will vary, but should
   involve a way to carry the food.
4. Chri<u>s</u> ha<u>s</u> a new <u>puppy</u>.